A Child's First Library of Learning

Animal Friends

TIME-LIFE BOOKS • ALEXANDRIA, VIRGINIA

Contents

? Why Do Dogs Sniff All Over the Place?

ANSWER When you take your dog for a walk it will sniff around places like the bottom of walls and telephone poles. It is smelling places where other dogs have urinated. The smell that a dog leaves is called a scent. This tells a dog when another dog was there and if it was bigger or smaller, stronger or weaker. When your dog has learned all this it will make its own scent by urinating there. That tells other dogs that this territory belongs to your dog.

How Other Animals Mark Their Territory

The mountain goat has a smelly fluid that comes from under its eyes. It rubs this on trees or rocky ledges.

A bear leaves its scent on a tree by rubbing its bottom against it or by urinating or leaving droppings.

An otter marks its territory by leaving droppings on dead trees or rocks near the river in which it lives.

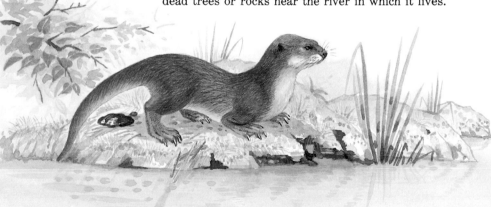

● To the Parent

An animal marks its territory with scent to avoid fights with other animals of the same species. Except for animals that live in groups, almost all animals have their own territory. They take the area around their nest or hole for their own use and drive off any animal of their species that tries to enter it. In addition to marking their territory with scent, they call to other animals that might enter it to warn them.

⚇ Why Do Dogs Wag Their Tails?

(ANSWER) Dogs use their tails to tell you how they feel. A dog wags its tail when it is happy. Sometimes we use our bodies to tell people how we feel. When we are very happy we might show others by jumping up and down or by clapping our hands.

A dog wags its tail when it is happy.

If it is suspicious or watchful its tail stands straight up.

When it is very angry, its tail will stick straight out behind it.

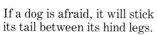
If a dog is afraid, it will stick its tail between its hind legs.

And to show you that it knows you are its master, it will roll on its back like this.

How Do Other Animals Show That They Are Angry or Happy?

When a cat is angry or afraid it arches its back to make itself look bigger.

When a horse is angry it puts back its ears and curls its lips so as to show its teeth. But when it is happy it will lift its tail high in the air.

But when a cat is happy it purrs.

When a rabbit is happy it twists its body as it hops along.

A chimpanzee's face shows its feelings

An angry face

A laughing face

● **To the Parent**

For many animals the tail is the most expressive part of the body. While dogs wag their tails when they are happy, a cat expresses itself differently. When it is feeling conceited or proud, its tail will stick straight up into the air. Certain monkeys will put their tails up and swish them to and fro to frighten off a potential enemy. Horses hold their tails high when they are feeling full of spirit and want to race around.

7

Why Do Dogs Bark at Strangers?

ANSWER Long ago dogs lived in packs. If a stranger came around, one dog would bark and warn the others, and they would attack the stranger. Your dog thinks of you as one of its pack. If a stranger comes near you or your home your dog will bark to keep him away.

A dog guards its home ground against strangers and won't let anyone it doesn't know near it.

A dog that is chained up has a very small home ground and will guard it even more fiercely. That is why it barks so loudly at strangers.

Times When Dogs Bark

■ When they are puppies

Puppies are careful because they are learning. They will bark at anything they don't understand to frighten it.

■ When they are hungry

A dog barks when you have forgotten to fill its food dish.

■ Just to call you

A dog will bark to let you know it wants something.

■ When they are happy

A dog knows when you are going to take it for a walk and barks loudly.

■ When they are unhappy or lonely

A dog will howl to let you know it feels bad.

● To the Parent

In the animal world there is social space, a region that is like the animal's territory, and personal space, which is the small area very close to the animal. If a person or animal enters an animal's social space, the animal may just growl a warning. An example is a dog growling as strangers approach a home. If the invader then persists and enters the animal's personal space, the animal may attack the invader and attempt to drive it out. Though a dog may fight to protect its space, it will allow persons that it knows to enter it without harm.

9

Do Dogs and Cats Have Dreams?

ANSWER Yes, dogs and cats dream just like we do. Sometimes a dog will whimper or cry when it is asleep. And sometimes it will wag its tail or move its legs as if it were running. This could mean that it is having a dream, perhaps one about fighting or playing.

A dog will sometimes wet its bed while it is asleep. It probably does this when it is dreaming.

When Do Dogs and Cats Sleep?

Pet dogs sleep a lot. But they jump right up if they hear a strange sound. Cats sleep during the daytime. At night they wander around outside and explore in different places.

REX

● **To the Parent**

Checking the brain waves of dogs and cats as they sleep has shown that they actually do have dreams just as humans do. A dog whimpering as it sleeps may be a sign that it is dreaming. When they are having a dream the pattern of their brain waves is almost the same as when they are awake. Dogs and cats are nocturnal animals, though dogs have adapted to human habits and now sleep a lot at night. Cats, on the other hand, still preserve much of their nocturnal nature, and therefore they stay out much or all of the night and sleep during the day.

Why Are Cats' Claws Sharp?

 Cats need sharp claws to catch mice and to climb trees. The claws are growing all the time. When the cat sharpens them the old claws are worn away and new nail moves up from underneath to take their place. So cats sharpen them to get rid of the old part and to always keep them sharp.

ANSWER 2 At home your pet cat may leave its claw marks on your family's best furniture. It also sharpens its claws on the trees around the edge of your garden. These claw marks are one of the ways it marks out its territory.

When cats were still wild they would mark their home ground with their claw marks on trees.

Some Animals Use Tree Trunks to Sharpen Things

Animals keep their horns, claws and teeth sharp to catch the food they eat or to defend themselves.

Leopard

This catlike animal sharpens its claws on trees.

Deer

Male deers' horns are called antlers. They rub them to remove the soft felt covering.

Wild boar

Wild boars have tusks. They keep them sharp by rubbing them against trees.

● **To the Parent**

Cats have claws that they can retract or extend. Dogs' claws are not retractable. Dogs' and cats' claws differ because they hunt in different ways. A dog hunts its prey by chasing it down. It could not catch it if its feet slipped during the chase, which is why a dog's claws are extended. Cats creep up on their prey, so they must be very quiet. For this reason nature has provided them claws that slide up into a kind of sheath. The very soft pads on the undersides of their paws enable cats to sneak up on their prey without making a sound.

❓ Why Do Cats Use Dirt To Cover Their Droppings?

ANSWER Cats are very clean animals. They like to keep the area where they live clean, so they cover their urine or their droppings with earth. They don't do this outside their territory because leaving their scent out there tells other cats that they have been there.

A cat covers its droppings with earth

Most cats have regular places to sleep in the daytime.

When cats relieve themselves in their own territory, they always cover their urine or their droppings with earth.

14

▼ Cats have special places where they all meet

▼ Cats can walk along walls easily

come
his way
often.

Outside their own territory cats do not bother to cover up their droppings or the places where they urinate.

● **To the Parent**

The area where animals habitually carry out their activities is called their territory, and they will defend it against intrusion by animals they consider to be rivals. Dogs appear to be covering their droppings and their urine with dirt, but actually they are making marks in the ground with their claws. These marks, together with the scent they leave, are to let other dogs know that this is their territory. Cats are more social and have places where any number of cats meet at night.

❓ Why Do Cats' Eyes Glow in the Dark?

ANSWER Cats move around at night, so they must be able to see in the dark. Where humans can see nothing at all, cats can still see. A cat's eyes take in the tiniest bit of light. Inside the eye the light is reflected backward and forward. That is the reason that their eyes glow brightly in the dark.

My eyes don't glow like a cat's!

Some Others Whose Eyes Glow in the Dark

Most of these creatures hunt their prey at night.

Owls can catch small animals even when there is almost no light. They have very, very sharp ears.

Martens are good at climbing trees. They prey on bats and squirrels.

Snakes sleep in holes in the ground during the day They come out at night to hunt frogs and other prey.

Foxes prowl around at night looking for food.

● **To the Parent**

The pupils of cats' eyes change to control the amount of light that enters the eye. They narrow to tiny slits in bright sunlight but widen to large orbs when it is dark. That is why cats see so well in the dark. In addition there is an area behind the retina that reflects light, and that is why cats' eyes appear to glow in the dark. Actually what you see is merely a reflection of what light there is, and not the cat's eyes glowing. A cat's eyes will not glow in total darkness because there is no light for them to reflect.

Why Do Cats Purr?

ANSWER Cats love to be stroked. When you stroke them they purr, and the sound seems to come from deep in their throats. That's because they're saying that it feels good. And if you stop stroking them they will come and rub themselves against you and purr to tell you not to stop. Purring is the cat's way of getting you to pet it.

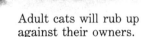

Adult cats will rub up against their owners.

Kittens get their mothers to wash their fur for them.

When kittens are hungry, they purr so their mother will give them milk.

Do Other Animals Also Cuddle Their Young?

The young of other animals do different things to get their mothers to play with them. They might lick their mother's fur or roll on their back in front of her so she will play with them.

Dogs lick your hands and face to get you to pet them.

▲ Cubs of the brown bear live with their mother until they are two or three years old.

▲ Kits love to play with the mother fox.

● **To the Parent**

When cats purr it generally means that they are feeling happy and contented. They probably have much the same feeling that we have when we are talking happily with some of our friends or neighbors. Kittens first start to purr about the time that they begin drinking milk from their mother. It is believed that purring in adult cats is a transfer to their human owners of the expression of affection that they learned as kittens.

▲ Baby monkeys are terribly spoiled by their mothers

❓ Why Are Rabbits' Ears Long?

ANSWER ❶ Those long ears give rabbits extra sharp hearing. And they need to hear well. Rabbits are weak animals. If an enemy comes near they must hide or run away at once. Their big ears help them hear even the softest sound of footsteps.

Tame rab

TRY THIS

Try putting the palms of your hand behind your ears. You can hear sounds much more clearly now, can't you? Maybe you can even hear the sound of a little breeze blowing that you didn't hear before.

MINI-DATA

Rabbits' ears turn in any direction: right, left, front or rear. That lets them hear sounds all around them.

ANSWER 2 Another reason that rabbits have long ears is to keep them from getting too hot. They can't sweat like we can, so when they are running away from an enemy they stick their ears straight up. Rabbits have a lot of blood in their ears, and as they run the wind cools that blood. The blood flows through their body, helping to keep it cool.

❓ What Do Some of the Other Animals Do To Keep Themselves from Getting Too Hot?

Dogs stick their tongues out and pant, and that cools them off.

Horses and human beings sweat, and that helps them stay cool.

Elephants flap their ears. The blood vessels in them catch the breeze, and that makes them cool.

▼ A polar bear cools off with a swim.

● **To the Parent**

A rabbit's long ears have two important functions: they not only give it its extremely sharp hearing but also act as a thermostat to keep the rabbit cool. A rabbit escaping from an enemy will have its ears stuck straight up in the air. Its ears catch the breeze as it runs, and this will cool the blood in the blood vessels in the ears. White rabbits have pink eyes. The inside of their ears is pink, too. This is because the tissue is so transparent the blood in the blood vessels shows through.

❓ Why Can Chimpanzees Do Tricks?

ANSWER Chimpanzees are very clever animals. They watch people and copy what they do. Because they are so smart, chimps can learn to do many things. People can teach them to ride a bicycle. Chimps can also learn to say words using sign language.

I'm quite clever, you know!

Other Animals That Can Do Tricks

Many animals can be taught to do tricks. Gorillas are as smart as chimpanzees. Some sea creatures like whales and dolphins are very smart too. Dogs and seals are not as smart, but they can learn tricks quickly.

▲ **Dogs.** They are very tame and learn quite fast.

▲ **Sea lions.** These are extremely smart and tame easily.

▲ **Dolphins.** They're friendly and respond well to humans.

● To the Parent

Apes, which include the chimpanzee and the gorilla, are among the most intelligent species in the animal kingdom. This is because they not only have larger brains than other animals, but the section of the brain concerning intelligence is second only to man's in size. Chimpanzees can figure out how to use tools and other implements without being taught. For example they will make use of a stem of grass when they raid the nests that ants have built. They push the stem of grass through the ant-hill entrance, scoop out the ants with it and eat them.

❓ Why Are Some Monkeys' Bottoms Red?

ANSWER Like us, monkeys have a lot of tubes in their bodies that are called blood vessels. Blood travels through these tubes to reach different parts of the body. Monkeys have a lot of these tubes in their bottoms, and it is the blood in the tubes that make their bottoms red. The skin on a monkey's bottom is also very tough, and that is another reason that it looks red.

Blood is what makes it red.

Some monkeys have hard pads on their bottoms that are just like cushions for them when they sit in the tops of trees.

Soft Bottoms Too

Monkeys that sleep in nests usually don't have hard pads to protect their bottoms.

We are all very clever!!

▲ **Gorillas.** They build large nests of leaves and branches.

▲ **Orangutans.** Their nests of branches are in the treetops.

▲ **Chimpanzees.** They also build nests high up in the trees.

● **To the Parent**

Some monkeys have red bottoms and faces because of the blood concentrated in the blood vessels there. Those that sleep in treetops are born with hard pads on their bottoms that serve as cushions. They can sleep on branches without discomfort. In some species, a particularly red bottom can be a signal that it's time for mating.

? What Do Lion Cubs Eat?

ANSWER When they are born, lion cubs drink milk from their mother. While they are still small, their mother gives them some of the food that she has caught. From the time they are about two years old until they are about three they learn how to hunt food and provide for themselves. Their mother, the lioness, teaches them.

▲ Lion cubs drinking their mother's milk

Don't Lions Get Ill If They Eat Only Meat?

No, not usually. That is because lions hunt animals that eat only grass. The stomach and intestines of these animals are filled with the nourishing things that come from grass. And lions eat these stomachs and intestines along with the rest, and that keeps them in good health even though they eat only meat. If a lion should get a bit sick it will eat grass, and that will make it feel better.

● **To the Parent**

When they are first born lion cubs are raised on milk from their mother. When they are weaned they start to eat meat that their mother has caught. The very first turn at the kill goes to the male. When the lion has eaten his fill, it is the turn of the lioness. The lion cubs eat last of all. The internal organs, including the stomach and entrails, of herbivores are rich in nutrients, including partially digested grass, vitamins and other elements, which cannot be obtained by eating meat alone.

? Why Are Elephants' Trunks So Long?

ANSWER Elephants' trunks are noses, but they are also like our hands. They can wave them about and pick up things with them. They use them to pull up grass that they eat and to drink water while they are standing up. If elephants didn't have such long trunks, they would probably have to kneel down to eat and drink.

■ How Jumbo drink

Elephants drink by drawing water up into their trunk, then shooting it back into their mouth.

Uses of the Trunk

Grown elephants use their trunks to rescue baby elephants that have gotten into trouble. They pick them up with their trunk and carry them to safety. They usually do not use the trunk for fighting.

Tip of the trunk ▶

An elephant uses the tip of its trunk the way we use fingers.

It can lift its trunk high and pick up various odours.

It can carry its baby with its trunk.

It can call to other elephants with its trunk.

It can pick leaves off trees with it.

It can drive away small enemies.

It can pick up all sorts of things.

● **To the Parent**

An elephant is able to move its long trunk freely because there are no bones in it. It uses its trunk as human beings use their hands for pulling up grass and tearing leaves off trees, for picking up things and even for carrying its young. It makes its shrill, piercing trumpeting sound with its trunk. And it can even be taught to throw a ball with its trunk. It also uses its trunk to drink with, sucking up water and shooting it into its mouth, and to wash with by shooting it over its back. Because of the important role the trunk plays, an elephant will take great care that its trunk doesn't get injured. That is why it hardly ever uses its trunk in fights.

Why Do Giraffes Have Long Necks?

ANSWER 1 Giraffes have long necks so they can catch sight of their enemies quickly. With its long neck and long legs the giraffe is the tallest of all animals. Giraffes are so tall that they can quickly spot their fiercest enemies.

Wow! This is sure high!

I can see a long way.

You often find herds of zebra and herds of giraffe together. This is because the giraffe quickly spot an enemy that comes near. Their alarm warns the zebras too.

ANSWER ❷ The giraffe's long neck also lets it eat the leaves on tall trees. It grasps the leaves with its long tongue, pulls them off and eats them.

▲ **There's its tongue**

■ Giraffes are swift

A grownup must run eight steps to go as far as a giraffe does in one stride.

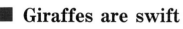

A grown-up pedaling a bicycle as fast as he could would not be able to catch a giraffe that was running away from an enemy.

■ Drinking is a problem

Because of their long necks and long legs, giraffes have a hard time getting a drink.

We don't have any problems when we drink.

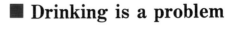

● **To the Parent**

Adult giraffes stand as tall as 20 feet (6 m). When fleeing from an enemy they take tremendously long strides, attaining speeds of 30 miles an hour (48 km/h) and holding that pace for long distances. Their great height lets them sight their enemies early and flee. They rarely fall prey to lions; in fact giraffes have been reported to have attacked lions with their powerful legs and hooves, and even to have broken a lion's jaw.

❓ Whose Horns?

■ A rhinoceros's

Rhinoceroses live on the grasslands in hot countries. If something makes them angry they will attack it and toss it into the air with their horns.

■ A water buffalo's

These animals love to pass the time cooling off in the water.

■ A mountain goat's

This one likes to live among rocks and on ledges high up in the mountains.

■ A moose's

Moose look like they have horns, but they don't. Moose have antlers. This moose lives in North America. It eats marsh grasses and leaves off trees.

■ A giraffe's

Giraffes are very tall, but their horns are very short. Mostly they eat leaves from the trees, but they also eat grass.

■ A bighorn sheep's

Their name comes from their horns. They are twice as big as an ordinary sheep. This one is very old, as its large horns show.

● **To the Parent**

The moose is the largest member of the deer family. The bull moose has antlers as much as six feet (1.8 m) across and weighing 45 pounds (20 kg). Both the male and female rhinoceros have horns. There are many kinds of sheep. Some have horns, and others do not, regardless of sex. Some animals, such as the giraffe, have hair covering their horns.

❓ Why Does a Baby Kangaroo Live in a Pouch?

ANSWER A mother kangaroo produces milk inside her pouch. A baby kangaroo stays inside its mother's pouch to drink her milk. When the baby kangaroo gets bigger it will come out of the pouch. But if an enemy appears, or something scares the baby, it hurries back to the pouch, where it feels safe and warm.

I'll bet it's nice and snug inside that little pouch.

▲ **A tiny feeder**

A baby kangaroo inside the pouch drinking its mother's milk.

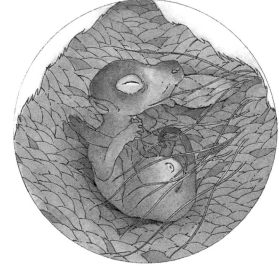

▲ As it feeds on mother's milk the baby grows larger.

Before long the baby is peeping out of the pouch and even nibbling grass along with its mother.

The mother kangaroo has a powerful kick and will use it to protect the offspring riding in her pouch.

When it is larger the baby will leave the pouch but will return occasionally.

Other Pouched Animals

▲ **Koala.** A mother and cub in the forests of Australia.

▲ **Flying squirrel.** Flying through the trees with baby.

● To the Parent

Baby kangaroos are totally without hair and are no more than .8 inch (2 cm) long at birth. After birth the baby finds its way to the mother's pouch and attaches itself to a teat. It will remain there suckling for about six months before it first pokes its head out. A koala lives in its mother's pouch when it is born, then clings to her back for another year or two after it leaves the pouch. Animals whose young are born prematurely and nurtured in pouches are marsupials. They are most commonly found in Australia and its neighboring islands.

? What Do Pandas Like to Eat?

ANSWER Pandas like to eat bamboo grass and bamboo shoots. And they really love the new bamboo sprouts that come out in the spring. In a zoo pandas will also eat apples and sweet corn. In their wild home pandas will eat small birds, snakes and river fish.

▲ **Pandas love these little bamboo sprouts**

Pandas' Life in the Wild

Pandas come from the mountains of China. The bamboo they love is plentiful there.

Pandas eat the leaves of bamboo and bamboo shrubs.

Pandas are good climbers.

They rub their bottoms on trees to leave their scent and tell other pandas that this is their territory.

Pandas usually live alone. They do not seem to enjoy company.

● To the Parent

There are only about 1,000 pandas living in the wild in the interior of China. The panda is a protected species, and there are surveys underway on its ecology and living habits. It is now believed that pandas do not hibernate. They appear instead to continue to feed all winter, eating right on through most of the night. They live alone except during the mating season.

? Why Do Goats Eat Paper?

ANSWER Goats eat grass and the leaves of trees. Paper is made from wood, and when a goat smells paper, it thinks it is something to eat. If the paper has print on it, it will contain printer's ink and probably other chemicals, and if a goat eats too much of that it may get a tummyache.

Some of the Goats

Other members of the goat family also eat grasses and leaves.

Goats love climbing and are often seen on the tops of hills.

▲ **Mountain goats.** These live in herds in rocky, mountainous areas. Domestic goats were probably tamed from these animals thousands of years ago.

▲ **Pygmy goats.** They're tiny and give milk. They also climb trees.

▲ **Long-eared goats.** Just look at those ears and that coat!

▶ **Milking goats**
Their milk is especially rich.

• To the Parent

There is nothing strange about goats eating paper since it is made from pulp, which is vegetable fiber. They digest it too. Goats have a very strong digestive system, and they are able to digest vegetation that other farm animals would not touch.

▶ **Alpine goats**
These are also kept for milking.

Why Do Mice Gnaw on Hard Things?

ANSWER A mouse's front teeth never stop growing. They must keep wearing them down, so they gnaw on hard things. If they didn't do that their teeth would keep growing until they couldn't close their mouth.

My teeth have become so long I can't eat anything.

When a mouse gnaws something its top teeth bite into it and press down hard. At the same time its bottom teeth push upwards and shave off a little bit at a time.

A mouse has such strong teeth that it can even nibble things made of concrete and metal.

A Mouse's Body

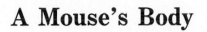

Mice can walk across ropes by keeping their balance with their long tails.

They can crawl into the smallest spaces. As long as they can get their head in, the rest of their body will follow.

When standing on their hind legs they support their body with their tails.

Mice have weak eyes. They find their way by touching the wall or the floor with their long whiskers.

They don't get sick even if they eat food that has gone bad.

Cold does not bother them.

Other Animals Whose Teeth Grow Fast

Rabbits

Squirrels

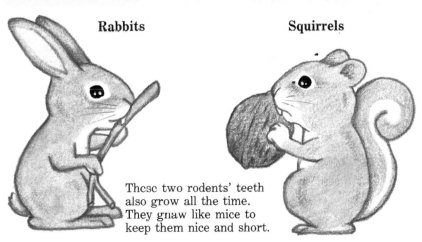

These two rodents' teeth also grow all the time. They gnaw like mice to keep them nice and short.

41

? Why Do Moles Live in the Ground?

(ANSWER) Moles live on earthworms, mole crickets and the young of other insects living in the soil. It makes things easier for moles if they live in the ground where they can find all the things they like to eat. Moles have lived underground for so long that their bodies have become perfectly suited to living there. They are also safe there because so few of their natural enemies also live underground.

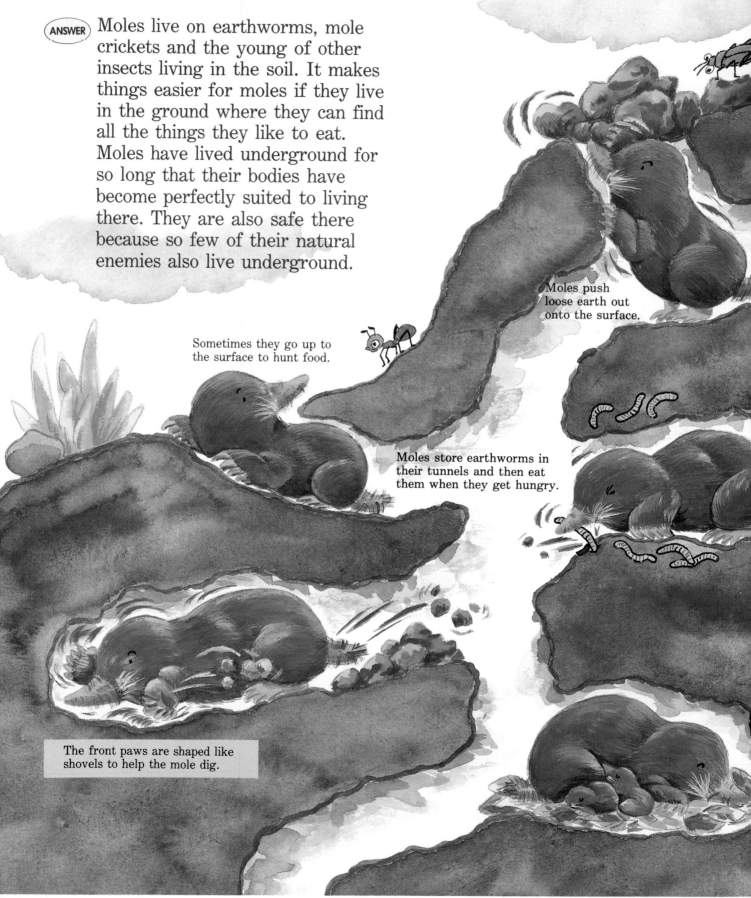

Moles push loose earth out onto the surface.

Sometimes they go up to the surface to hunt food.

Moles store earthworms in their tunnels and then eat them when they get hungry.

The front paws are shaped like shovels to help the mole dig.

They line their nests with grass and leaves.

Moles are almost totally blind, so they hunt food with their nose.

Moles have their babies in the nest.

● **To the Parent**

There is a belief that moles will die if they are exposed to sunlight for too long, but that is not true. They will die if they are captured and kept without food for more than three hours, and this may have caused the mistaken belief that they die if they get too much sunlight. Also they might die from shock if left too long in an exposed space or if most of their body is not in constant contact with some kind of surface.

Why Does the Camel Have a Hump?

(ANSWER) The camel stores a lot of fat inside its hump. Camels live in the desert, and there it might sometimes take days to find food or water. At times like these a camel lives by using up the nutrients stored in its hump.

There are camels with only one hump, but some have two humps.

When a camel hasn't eaten or drunk anything for a long time its hump will get smaller and smaller.

Camels can drink a LOT of water at one time. They don't drink often.

Camels don't need to drink water if they can find grass to eat. When they find plenty to eat, their hump will grow back to its normal size.

● **To the Parent**

The dromedary of West Asia and North Africa has only one hump. The Bactrian camel of Central Asia has two. Both can go for long periods without food or water by living off the fat of their humps and the water in their bodies. During those periods their hump gets smaller. When it reaches an oasis the ordinary camel will consume many gallons of water at one go,

❓ What Do Bats Eat?

ANSWER There are many kinds of bats, and they eat different things. Many eat flying insects, which they catch at night. To catch them they use their voices the way a plane uses radar.

Small bats live on insects. They come out at dusk to search for their food.

Fruit bats. These bats, which eat mostly fruit and nuts, are quite a bit larger than the ones that eat insects.

46

There Are Some Bats That Eat Other Things

There are many kinds of bats in the world. Here are some of them.

Fish-eating bats. These live in Mexico and Brazil. They come out at night and fish.

Long-tongued bats. They live in warm places. They drink nectar and eat pollen, which they collect with their long tongues.

Vampire bats. These also live in South America. They suck blood from living animals.

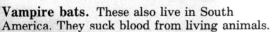

Frog-eating bats. These live in Panama. Their favorite food is the frogs they catch.

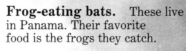

Bats are not birds. They are mammals and give birth to their own young. Their wings are made of a thin membrane stretched across a bony frame a little bit like your arm.

● **To the Parent**

There are many kinds of bats in the world. These are not birds but mammals. Usually bats live in caves or other dark places, coming out in the open at dusk to hunt the insects that are one of their major foods. But bats eat many other things: some eat fruit, others hunt frogs and some of them, called vampire bats, seek out animals and drink their blood.

? How Do Snakes Crawl?

(ANSWER) Snakes have scales under their bellies. Some use these scales to help them move forward.

■ They slither

Snakes slither along from side to side to go straight ahead.

■ They climb

Snakes that climb trees like this one move their body from branch to branch like this.

Snakes Can Swim Too

Snakes are good swimmers. They swim by moving their body from side to side in the water like they crawl.

48

● **To the Parent**

Snakes have long, thin bodies. In the place of legs they have scales that envelop their bodies and help them to go forwards. Some, like the Indian python, erect the scales to move, but others move by stretching, then contracting their bodies. A number of them move by undulating their bodies, always with the entire body touching the ground. Snakes lay eggs in the ground, where the heat of the earth hatches them. As they grow their skin becomes too tight, so they shed it and leave it behind. A new skin is there to take the old one's place.

Snakes Come From Eggs

▼ As a snake grows, its skin gets tight, so it sheds it.

49

❓ Can Birds See at Night?

ANSWER Birds like chickens, sparrows and crows can't see on a dark night. Such birds would bump into things if they flew at night, so they roost quietly.

Starlings return to their nesting place at night.

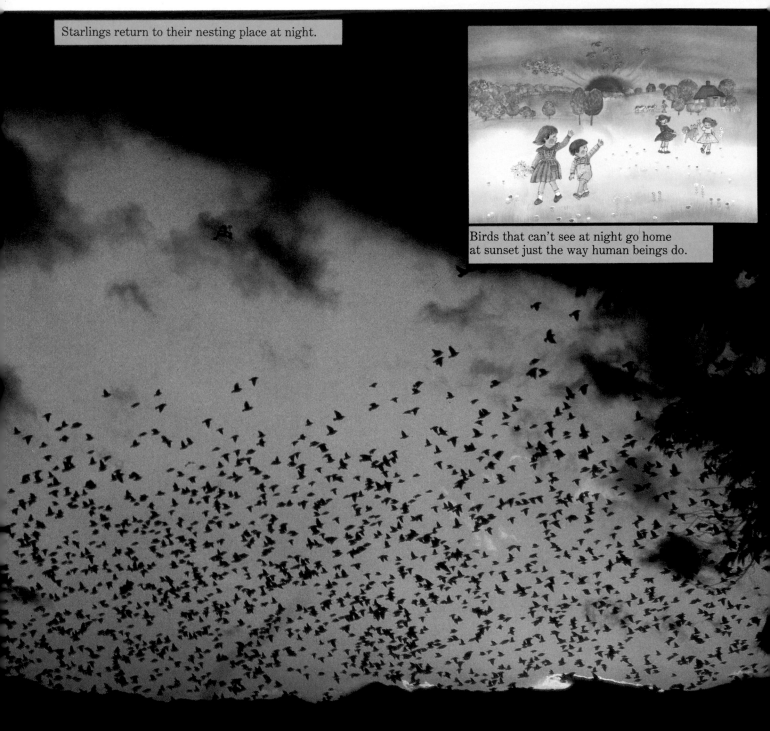

Birds that can't see at night go home at sunset just the way human beings do.

Some Birds See at Night

Some birds can see very well at night, and most of them are quite good hunters. This kind of bird dozes during the day and comes out to hunt its prey at night.

▲ Night jars fly around during the night catching insects in their great big mouths.

▲ The owl, a mighty hunter, leaves its nest at night to go in search of mice and other prey.

Ducks fly around watery places at night in search of their food. At dawn they settle down to sleep.

● **To the Parent**

Most birds are commonly believed to suffer from night-blindness, but in fact there are quite a lot of birds that can see at night. Birds that cannot see in the dark have fewer of the rods that are sensitive to light and dark in their retinas. Birds that can see in the dark find it safer to move around at night, so they spend their days drowsing in the shade and search for food after dark. Many migrating birds also fly at night and sleep in the daytime.

51

Why Do Eggs Turn Into Chicks When They Are Kept Warm?

ANSWER When the hen sits on the eggs it warms them, and a chick starts to grow in each. In 21 days the chick will be big enough to break out of the shell by itself.

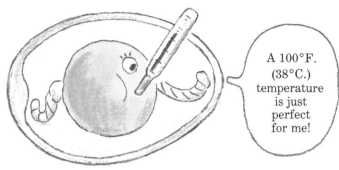

A 100°F. (38°C.) temperature is just perfect for me!

She wishes her chicks would hurry up and hatch.

The mother hen checks her eggs now and then. She moves the eggs around to try to keep the temperature of them as even as she possibly can.

Her chicks have hatched and left their shells!

All Birds Keep Their Eggs Warm to Make Them Hatch

After laying their eggs, birds keep them warm until the baby chicks are hatched. Sometimes the mother will do this all by herself, sometimes the father bird will do it and sometimes the two will take turns.

The mother crow hatches the eggs all by herself.

The mother and father sparrow take turns at keeping the eggs warm.

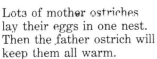

Lots of mother ostriches lay their eggs in one nest. Then the father ostrich will keep them all warm.

Penguins usually lay only one egg. With their feet they hold it up among their stomach feathers to keep it warm.

⍰ Why Do Chickens Take Sand Baths?

ANSWER Chickens take sand baths to keep clean and free of bugs. They rub themselves around on the ground to get a lot of sand all throughout their feathers. When they shake themselves to get the sand out, bugs that were hiding among their feathers fall out too.

Louse

Dirt

Louse

What Do Some of the Other Birds Do To Keep Themselves Clean?

Pheasants give themselves sand baths the way chickens do. Most other birds wash in water to get rid of bugs and dirt.

Sparrows take both water baths and sand baths

■ Cleaning with ants

One jay crushes ants and puts them under its wings. The smell of the ants sticks to its body and keeps other insects away.

■ Smoking out bugs

Seagulls find bonfires and fly through their smoke. The bugs cannot stand the smoke. They must leave the gull or die.

● **To the Parent**

By giving themselves a sand bath, chickens are able to shake loose lice and other insects that have crawled between their feathers. Chickens, the other relatives of the pheasant and skylarks don't bathe in water because they hate getting their feathers wet, but they give themselves sand baths. Almost all other birds bathe in water before they oil their feathers.

? Why Don't Chickens Fly?

ANSWER Chickens used to fly when they lived in the wild. But they learned to live on the ground. Birds like the chicken or ostrich, which live on the ground, have smaller wings. The muscles in the wings are too weak for flying.

Are There Other Reasons That Chickens Cannot Fly?

ANSWER 1 With people feeding them and keeping them, they didn't have to worry too much about enemies, so they didn't really need to fly, and their muscles got too weak for flight.

ANSWER 2 Another reason is that they got fat and heavy. After people started keeping chickens they wanted to make them nice and plump so they would be good to eat. So they gave them a lot to eat, and with no exercise the chickens' wings became so weak that they could not lift those heavy bodies.

Grounded!

Awk! I'm stuffed!

● **To the Parent**

The ancestor of the domestic chicken is believed to be the red jungle fowl of Southeast Asia. Their long years of living in captivity have reduced their flying muscles to flabbiness, while at the same time their weight has increased so much that they are no longer able to fly. Even today, however, if they were kept in free range conditions they still might be able to fly a vertical distance of a few yards, but they would be quite unable to remain in the air for long periods.

❓ Why Do Swallows Nest Under Eaves?

(ANSWER) An eave is the lower edge of a roof that extends over the side of a building. Swallows build nests of straw and mud, and need places that are wide and flat. The space under eaves is like that. Eaves are safe too. Cats and big birds can't get in under them. Baby swallows will be safe until they are big enough to fly.

Do Other Birds Build Their Nests Around Houses?

Yes, there are other birds that build nests in or around houses. All birds look for a safe place to build nests, lay their eggs and hatch their young. The way they build their nests and the places that they build them may differ with the species of bird.

A starling's nest on a roof

Sparrows. They may build nests in the attics of houses.

Doves. These build their nests in tree branches.

Starlings. These try to find hollows in walls for nesting.

Great tit. They will build in mail boxes if they can.

● **To the Parent**

It is believed that swallows originally built their nests in crags and on cliff faces, but since people began to build houses birds have made use of them and now build their nests under the eaves of homes and other handy buildings like train stations. Birds build nests for the purpose of laying their eggs and raising their young and not to sleep in like mammals and other animals. Nesting material varies greatly with the bird species.

Why Do So Many Pigeons Live Near Big Buildings?

ANSWER Pigeons have learned to live in cities. In big buildings like churches there are lots of places to roost. There are also friendly people around, so the pigeons have plenty to eat.

Pigeons like to live in large flocks. If a flock stays near a church lost pigeons can find their way back to the flock easily. New pigeons often join the flock, so it keeps growing all the time. That's why the flocks have so many birds.

Come and join our flock!

Different Pigeons That You Might See in a Flock

Pigeons living in city buildings have come from many places to join the flock, so they are of various sizes and colors. Many people think that these pigeons are a nuisance and even unhealthy because of their droppings.

● **To the Parent**

Pigeons evolved from the rock dove of West Asia and temperate Europe. The names pigeon and dove are used interchangeably, though the latter generally is applied to smaller members of the family. The domestic pigeon and the street pigeon are the ones that generally inhabit the grounds of stations, churches and other public places. Pigeons almost always live in flocks.

❓ Did You Know That Pigeons Feed Milk to Their Babies?

ANSWER Baby pigeons are raised on milk. They get the milk from both their mother and father. The milk comes from the back of the adult pigeon's throat. The babies push their beaks down the parents' throats to get at the milk.

▼ **Baby turtledoves getting milk**

How Do Different Species of Birds Go About Raising Their Young?

Birds raise their young in all sorts of ways.

Cuckoo. It lays its egg in the bush warbler's nest. The warbler is tricked into thinking that the egg is its own, so it hatches it and then raises the baby.

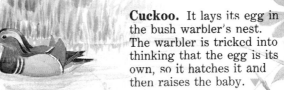

Mandarin duck. The only thing the father does is find a nest. The mother hatches the eggs and raises the chicks.

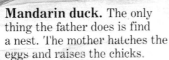

Painted snipe. The mother lays her eggs and then disappears. Father snipe hatches the eggs and raises the babies.

Reed warbler. She lays the eggs, hatches them and raises the chicks all by herself.

Reed bunting. If it is cold or raining this mother will keep her young ones warm and safe under her wings.

Plover. If an enemy approaches the nest, the plover will pretend that it has hurt itself and will lead the enemy away from the baby plovers.

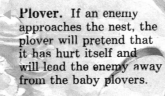

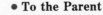

● **To the Parent**

For a few days after pigeon chicks are hatched the parents feed them on their own milk. This is a substance that comes from the bird's crop, a pouch-like enlargement close to the bird's throat where food is stored after partial digestion. Sometimes the mother cares for the chicks; sometimes that is the father's duty; sometimes both parents will share the duty

How Do Homing Pigeons Find Their Way Home?

The sun's over there, so home must be this way!

ANSWER A homing pigeon's body has a built-in "compass." It uses it to figure out which direction to go when heading home. When it's close to home a pigeon can recognize the landscape.

MINI-DATA

Long, long ago before there were telephones, people used these birds to carry messages. They were very useful since they were swifter than either horses or boats and could deliver the messages much faster.

Since they could carry messages, homing pigeons were also called carrier pigeons.

Homing pigeons have good memories and know their area extremely well.

❓ Why Are Parrots Able to Talk?

ANSWER A parrot has a large, thick tongue, not exactly like a human tongue, but it helps the bird talk. The parrot makes sounds like the ones it hears. It does not understand the words it says.

Dogs have large tongues but they are thin, not thick, so they cannot talk the way parrots do.

AH...

AH.. AH...

Are There Other Birds That Can Talk?

Yes, there are other birds that can talk just like parrots.
They not only talk as we do, they copy other things we do.

▲ **Myna bird.** These are clever at copying all sorts of things.

A myna bird can utter a sound just like a telephone ringing.

▲ **Gray starling**

▲ **Carrion crow**

▲ **Lovebirds**

● **To the Parent**

Parrots are members of a tropical or subtropical family of birds with hooked bills, brightly colored feathers and feet with two toes pointing backward and two forward. There are 315 species, ranging in height from 4 to 40 inches (10 cm to 1 m). Some learn to imitate human speech. Some other birds also develop this ability. They are mere mimics, however, and have no idea of the meaning of the words. They imitate not only human voices but also calls of other birds in the wild.

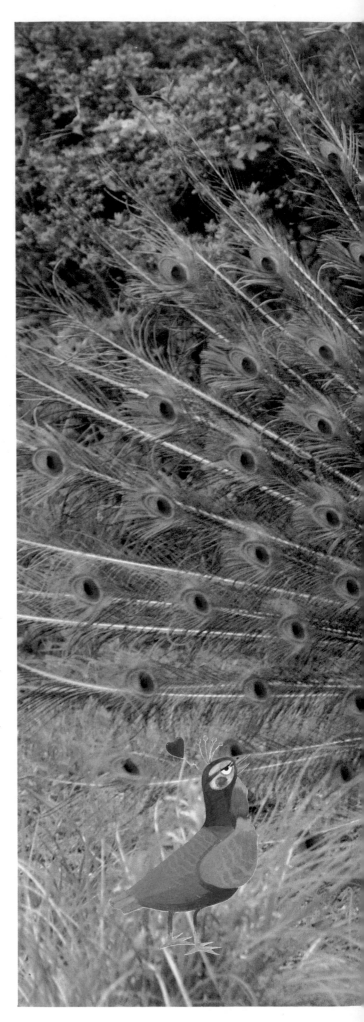

? Why Do Peacocks Fan Their Tails?

ANSWER It is only the male peacock that spreads his tail feathers into a fan. He does it when he meets a female. He tries to show her how handsome he is, and he wants to get her to like him by doing this.

▲ **A peahen.** The female is not colorful like the male.

How Do Swans Float on Water?

ANSWER Swans have many fleecy feathers set very close together. They preen and groom themselves all the time to keep the feathers coated with oil. That keeps water from wetting the feathers and lets the swans float.

Swans have oil in their body. They put it on their feathers with their beak.

After diving down into the water a swan beats its wings to shake all the water off of them.

A Swan's Life

■ An expert swimmer

Swans have webbed feet. That's one reason they are such good swimmers.

■ Swans hunt food all over

If they spot something that looks good to eat, it's tails up, heads down! Besides diving for food, swans also eat things floating on the surface of the water.

TRY THIS

Take two cotton balls, and soak one of them in oil. Put them into two glasses of water. Which one of them will float?

The one with the oil floated.

The one with no oil on it sank.

▲ **A mallard.** Its feathers shed water.

■ Sleeping on water

If they get drowsy, swans just put their head under their wing and doze off!

■ A running start

Swans have heavy bodies, so they run on the top of the water to pick up speed before they take off and fly into the air.

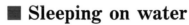

● **To the Parent**

Swans have fine, lush feathers. The birds groom their feathers constantly to keep them coated with oil so that they will repel water and the swans can float.

Why Do Cranes Have Such Long Bills?

ANSWER Cranes live in wet marshlands where there are many little pools of water. They live on grass seeds and grass shoots that fall into the water. They also feed on fish and frogs, which live in the water. Their long bills are very useful for picking food out of the ponds and marshes where they live.

Picking seeds from the water.

Catching a frog in its bill.

It's just like chopsticks!

A Variety of Beaks

Different birds have different beaks, depending on the type of food they eat and the way they go about catching it.

Flamingo. This bird feeds on small creatures living in the water. It scoops them up in a spoonlike bill that separates the food and water.

Eagle. It uses its great curved beak to tear pieces of flesh off the small animals it catches.

▲ **Spotted woodpecker.** It picks insects out of trees, using its hard, sharp-pointed beak to get at the morsels.

▲ **Sparrow.** This tiny brown bird has a thick, hard beak, which is very useful for breaking open seeds.

73

? Why Do Some Birds Fly in Formation?

ANSWER They don't get so tired that way. When one bird flaps its wings it makes a draft. Birds to the rear get help from this draft and don't have to fly so hard. Birds in front and rear change position now and then to help even up the work.

This makes flying a lot easier!

Geese flying in a V formation

Flying in formation makes it easier
for birds to flee from enemies. When
they are in nice straight lines they
can turn sharply in any direction
without bumping into other birds.
So if they meet an enemy, the entire
flock can change direction instantly.
And that is the way that they escape.

These birds can change
direction instantly
without bumping into
any of the other birds.

Smaller Birds Fly in Group Formation

Instead of the V formation smaller birds fly very close together
in a group formation. If a hawk or other enemy appears the flock
flees while the enemy is making up its mind what bird to attack.

● To the Parent

Large birds such as ducks and geese normally fly in a wedge
formation, while smaller ones such as starlings and thrushes
usually fly in close groups. The tips of flying birds' wings
create air currents, and it is believed that a bird flying
behind another can rest on the rising air currents and thus
not use so much energy. The V formation lets bigger birds
change directions suddenly without flying into one another.

❓ Don't Penguins Get Cold Living on the Ice?

ANSWER A penguin has lots of feathers, which grow very close together. They keep the penguin just as cozy as if it were wearing a fur coat. Penguins also have a lot of fat under their skin, as though they were wearing many clothes. That keeps the cold air from getting inside their bodies.

▲ Penguin chicks are covered with a fluffy fur coat when they are born, so they actually stay pretty warm.

We have a nice warm coat of feathers, sort of like a fur coat, so cold is not much of a problem for us penguins.

Some Other Animals That Live on the Ice

Many animals live on the ice at the North and South Poles. Though it is very cold there, their fat and fur keep them warm.

Seal

Walrus

Seals and walruses have bodies shaped sort of like penguins, don't they?

▲ **Polar bears.** They don't feel the cold much because of their pretty white coats.

● **To the Parent**

Galápagos penguins and Humboldt's penguins live in very warm areas, but most penguins are found in freezing climates. Ears and noses and other protuberances of animals living in the arctic regions tend to be shorter and less pronounced than those of animals living in warmer climates. Reduced surface area and thick fur or feathers control loss of body heat.

77

❓ What Are They Doing?

These big elephants are throwing dirt over their bodies. When they are covered with dirt it makes it hard for the insects to sting them.

Birds like this one are called cleaners because they clean insects off of animals and eat them. They help the animal by cleaning it; the animal helps the birds in return by furnishing their food.

◀ This beaver is carrying a branch, which it will use for building its dam.

◀ The sea otter is eating a clam, which it caught on the bottom of the seabed.

◀ The monkey is picking dirt and insects out of the hair of the other monkey.

Monkeys like to keep themselves clean, so they often groom one another like this.

● **To the Parent**

Grooming one another is useful in maintaining good relations among monkeys as well as for keeping their fur clean. The sea otter will float on its back with a stone on its stomach for breaking open shellfish and crabs to get the meat. Elephants give themselves dust baths to keep their hides covered with sand or dirt and keep parasites from living off their bodies.

? What Are All These Birds Doing?

▲ These cranes are dancing. They dance during mating season or at other times to amuse themselves.

▲ The bullheaded shrike, or butcher-bird, sticks a lizard it has caught on the thorn of a tree. This is the bird's way of saving it. When it is hungry it will eat the prey.

▲ These are baby crows. When they are hungry they open their mouths wide like this to get their mother to feed them.

● To the Parent

When a mother crow gets back to the nest the chicks all open their mouths wide, asking to be fed. The mother crow will give the food to the chick whose mouth is open widest. That is because she recognizes it as the hungriest chick in her brood. Male and female cranes frequently dance together. Often when a dance has begun, other cranes will gather around and join in.

Growing-Up Album

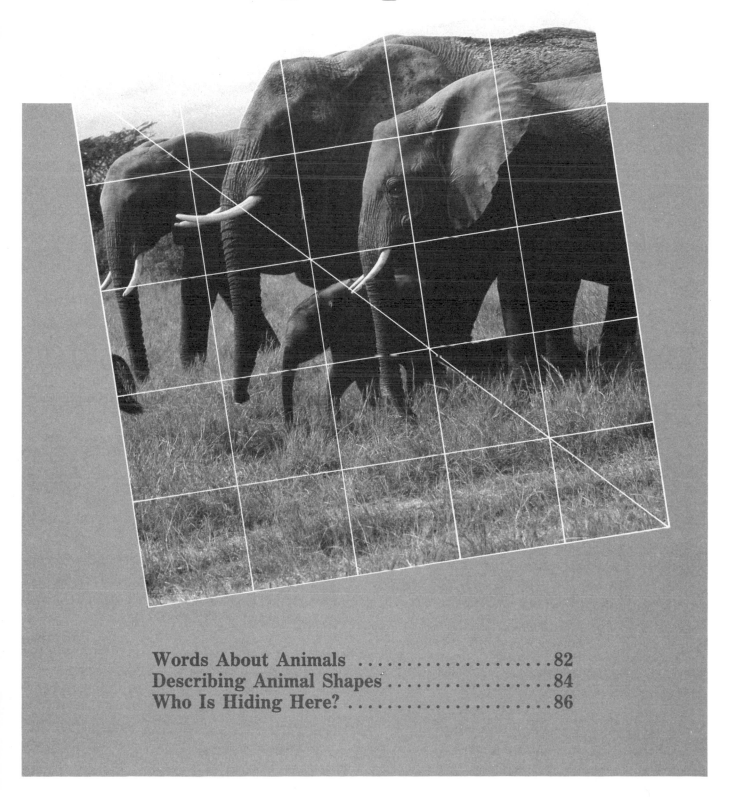

Words About Animals

How can we describe the sounds that animals make? Or the different ways that they move? Children often invent the most apt expressions. They create a great many novel and unexpected words that both surprise and amuse adults. It could be fun to make a list of some of these.

■ What sounds do they make?

Cow ⎯⎯⎯⎯⎯⎯⎯⎯

Horse ⎯⎯⎯⎯⎯⎯⎯⎯

Monkey

Dog

Cat

Chicks

Frog

Chicken

■ Other animal sounds

How do these animals move?

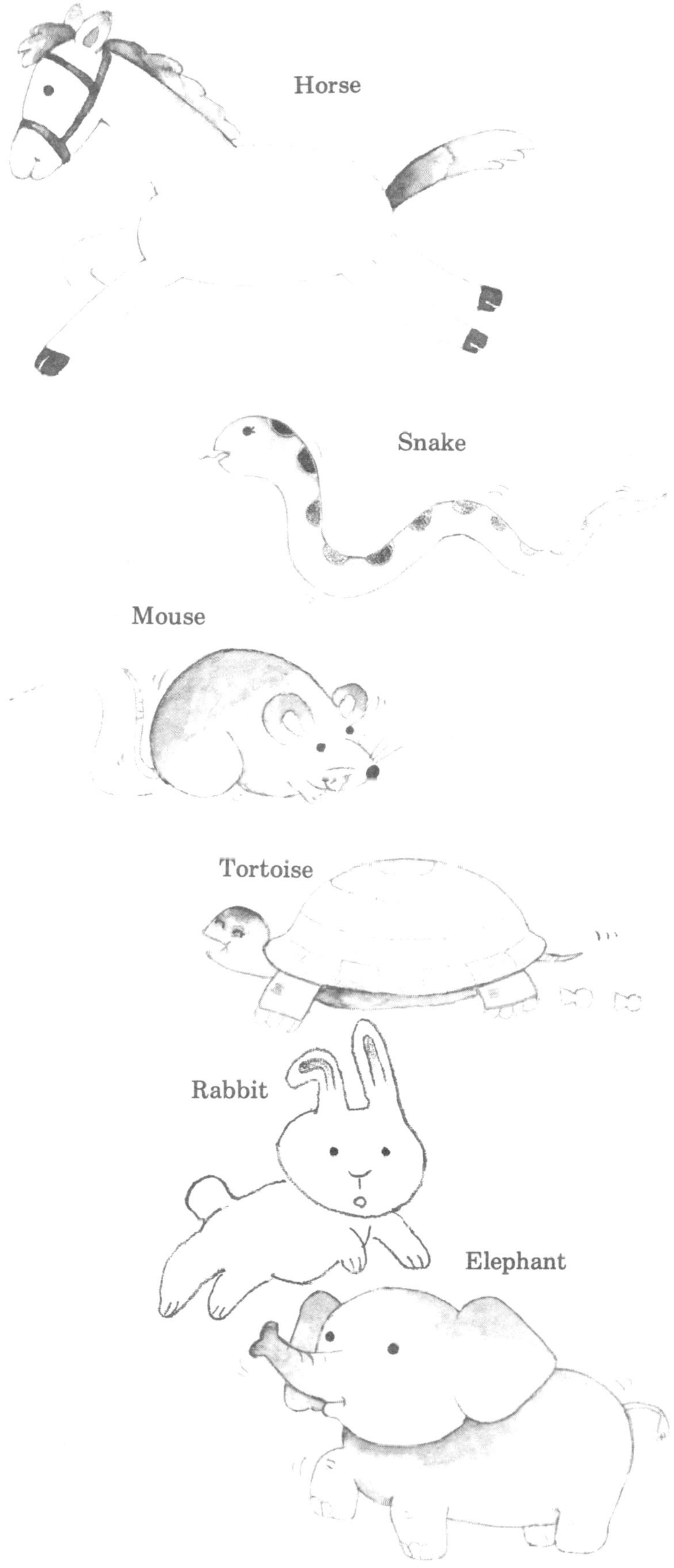

Horse

Snake

Mouse

Tortoise

Rabbit

Elephant

Describing Animal Shapes

We describe the shapes of different animals by giving examples and comparing them to things that children are familiar with. For instance we might say that an elephant's trunk is like a rubber hose, or that a giraffe's neck is like a crane. Children are often poetic and sometimes surprising, but they are never dull. Keeping a list of these expressions could be worthwhile.

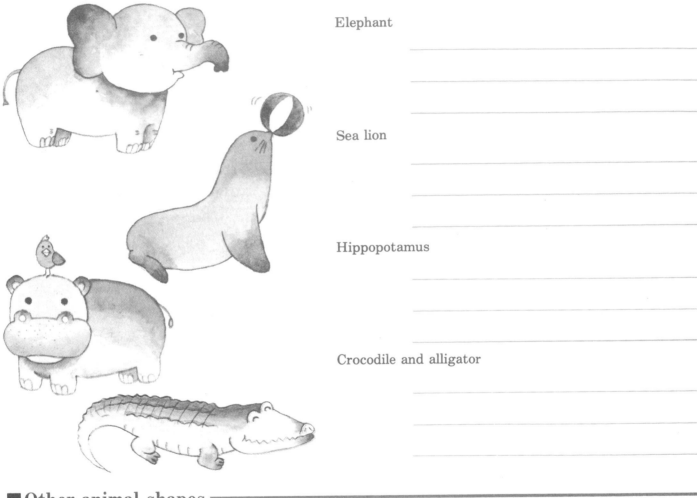

Elephant

Sea lion

Hippopotamus

Crocodile and alligator

■Other animal shapes

Rhinoceros

Lion

Penguin

Giraffe

Who Is Hiding Here?

There are quite a few animals and birds
hiding in this picture. Can you find them?